Elf Town

by Ginger England Burrows

This book is dedicated to my mother BJ England. "Thank you for making all our Christmases so wonderful, I love you!"

Santa Claus has so many elves that help him all year long by making toys for children all around the world and keeping track of the Naughty and Nice List. Every day, there are elves making and building toys that will be delivered to every child on earth on Christmas Eve night.

But where do they all live, and what do they do when they are not making toys or reporting back to Santa?

Santa made the elves their own special town called Elf Town, and this is where all Santa's elves live. This magical town sits in the valley directly below Santa's house and

workshops in the North Pole. Each elf has their own Christmas cottage, and each cottage is unique for each elf. The town is full of beautifully lit and decorated Christmas trees, and the elves change the decorations on the trees each month, and they always make sure to put

candy tinsel on the trees for the squirrels and reindeer to eat. In the center of their beautiful town, there are shopping boutiques of every sort, and the elves love to spend days shopping just like we do.

There are two huge dining halls in their town that serve up the most

scrumptious foods for the elves; one is named The Sugar Cookie, and the other one is named The Candy Cane. These dining halls are open all day and all night so the elves can get any food they want anytime they are hungry. They also have little Christmas Cafes throughout their special

SWEETIES CAFÉ

THE LOLLIPOP

MISTLETOE CAFÉ

town that serve up wonderful Christmas delights, desserts, and hot cocoa where the elves can go and be merry with friends.

Elf town also has a big year-round carnival. There are many fun rides, games, and treats at this carnival like cotton candy, candy apples, candy ribbon,

and snow cones of course;
the snow falls right into
the sweet, sugary cones,
and then the sweetest
flavors are poured onto
the snow to make the
perfect snow cones. The
elves also love to skate,
and they have a very large
ice-skating rink with an
elf DJ that plays all their
favorite Christmas music

to skate to. Sledding down the snowy hills is another favorite fun that the elves love to do. Once a month they have a sledding festival where the elves compete in teams to see who has the best sledding skills, but the reindeer games are their favorite competition. Once a year, all the elves get together

for the reindeer games. They practice their reindeer riding all year long to get into this competition to see who has the best reindeer riding skills. The categories are how fast the reindeer flies, how high the reindeer flies, and how many tricks the reindeer can do. Each elf has their

own reindeer, and they train with their reindeer all year to teach them skills for this competition. Their reindeer is also their pet, and it lives with them just as a dog or a cat live with you, and they also ride their reindeer to and from wherever they are going if it is too far for them to walk. The elves take incredibly good care of their reindeer and give them lots of love and feed them very well! The elves also love a good gift-wrapping contest, and they do this a lot throughout the year to see which elf can wrap a gift the fastest; prizes and awards are always included in elf contests.

Some of the elves love to decorate their sleighs by adding lights, garland, ornaments, bells, and other fancy things to it and they have meetups on the weekends at what is called a "sleigh meet" so they can show off their sleigh and see how other elves decorate theirs while they all mingle. They have

plays and concerts; elves love to act, sing, dance and play instruments, and they have a big art museum for the elves who love to draw, color, and paint. The most famous painting in the art museum is of a beautiful young elf girl named Annelisa and it was painted hundreds of years

ago by a famous elf artist named Leo.

In the summer, when it is not snowing, the elves love to have picnics and watch Christmas movies under the stars at their outdoor movie theatre. The younger elves have school classes that teach them toy making and every language in the

world, so they understand what all the children are saying.

Santa's elves always stay busy and have so much to do; they live a magical life of love, laughter, and fun. They always stay jolly and love to help each other. They love their reindeer, their cottages, and their beautiful Christmas town and always keep it decorated and sparkly clean. But the most important thing in the world to an elf is to make toys for children, making toys is what they love to do best. They get extremely excited and happy when they see the gleam in a child's eyes

when they finally open that special gift that was made especially for them. But there is one thing, and only one thing that makes Santa's elves happier, and that is when they get to walk into Santa's great big office, open his big book of names, and write YOUR name on his Nice List!

The End

Printed in the USA
CPSIA information can be obtained
at www.ICGtesting.com
CBHW051937180724
11797CB00031B/560